The Floral Gifts Project Book

Joanna Sheen

PHOTOGRAPHY BY JACQUI HURST

MEREHURST

Published in 1995 by Merehurst Limited,
Ferry House, 51–57 Lacy Road, Putney, London SW15 1PR

ISBN 1 85391 357 X

A catalogue record of this book is available from the British Library.

Edited by **Heather Dewhurst**
Designed by **Lisa Tai**
Styling by **Jacqui Hurst**

Typeset by Servis Filmsetting Ltd., Manchester
Colour separation by Global Colour, Malaysia
Printed in Singapore by Craftprint

Contents

ஃ

$\mathcal{I}$ntroduction

$\mathcal{F}$lowers make wonderful gifts for all age groups, and for both sexes. Although traditionally flowers have been given as gifts to women, there are many male gardeners who would love to receive a gift of plants or a bunch of flowers.

A gift made with dried flowers has the bonus of early preparation – you can make Christmas or birthday offerings well in advance, provided that they are kept fairly warm and dark to prevent any absorption of moisture or colour loss. If you plan to make quite a number of your own Christmas presents, any that can be made and tucked away are an invaluable help to finishing everything on time! Although some of the projects are aimed for specific occasions, with a small change here and there they can easily be adapted to suit many others. If you have a good collection of basic flower arranging items such as foam, containers, wires and ribbons, then a present can be made very quickly should the need arise.

Preparing flowers for gifts

Packaging is a very important part of making your own gifts. A pretty box or ribbon, some cellophane or a special container can raise a homemade display into a special handmade creation! If you spend a little extra time planning the presentation of your gift, your efforts will be amply rewarded by the appreciative comments when you hand over the present.

Collecting various items in advance is well worth doing. I have a deep drawer that is full of bits and pieces that may well be just what I'm looking for – one day! Seriously, though, a collection of boxes or ribbons, pretty paper and string, and other odds and ends can make present manufacturing much easier.

CARE OF FRESH FLOWERS

If you are planning to give a gift of fresh flowers, it is obviously important to have the best quality flowers that have been treated to last as long as possible. If you grow flowers for cutting in your garden, then these should be fresh and with proper conditioning should last well. Good quality flowers from a florist can last even longer as they are often grown to be long lasting. It is important to have a good source for your flowers as half-dead flowers will never make a good arrangement and your time will not have been used to its best advantage.

Once you get your flowers indoors, whether they are home-grown or from a florist, cut the bottom of the stalks at an angle and immerse the flowers in deep water overnight. This should give them a good long drink which should help them to last longer in your arrangements.

DRYING FLOWERS

Many flowers will dry just as well at home as in commercial drying kilns. Producing an arrangement that you have grown and dried yourself is very satisfying.

Collect the flowers you wish to dry on a bright, dry day and harvest them just before they reach their full maturity. Strip off some of the lower leaves and tie in small bunches, fixing them with a strong elastic band. It is important not to use string for this purpose as the stems shrink during the drying process and the bunch may fall and damage some of your precious blooms!

Hang these small bunches somewhere warm and dark, but with reasonable air circulation. A dry loft or attic can be ideal – a garage is not suitable as the night temperatures may be too low to be beneficial to the flowers. A spare bedroom or cupboard with the doors ajar can sometimes be a solution. Once the flowers are dry, they can be stored in boxes packed with tissue paper and kept at a reasonable temperature.

PRESSING FLOWERS

Preserving flowers in a press is an easy technique if all the basic pointers are followed. Many people use presses (often unsuccessfully) as children, but good pressing is only possible if a few basic rules are followed.

• Only collect perfect specimens that have begun to open that day – and only pick on a bright, dry day, preferably in the morning.

• Choose mainly thin or flat flowers, such as pansies, larkspur and lawn daisies, and avoid thick, lumpy specimens such as chrysanthemums and thick-centred daisies.

• Use clean, dry blotting paper and pads of dry newspaper in your press. Place a pad of newspaper at the bottom of the press and cover with a sheet of blotting paper. Lay a few flowers on the blotting paper, making sure they do not touch or overlap and then cover them with more blotting paper. Continue building alternate layers of newspaper and blotting paper with flowers between, until you have reached a maximum of ten layers.

Screw down the press as firmly as possible and leave in a warm place for about six to eight weeks – without looking inside!

• Once your pressed flowers are ready to use, store them in a warm, dark place so that the petals don't fade and to prevent re-absorption of moisture, which would cause the flowers to turn mouldy. Cellophane-fronted paper bags or blotting paper folders work well for storage.

Fresh, dried and pressed flowers make lovely gifts. Collect baskets, ribbons and doilies in advance.

Table centre

A combination of fresh and preserved material gives this table centre an unusual look, which can be changed very easily by adding new fresh flowers to the small displays on each side of the basket. The centre can be filled with chocolates, nuts or fruit.

Table centre

This arrangement is a useful way of combining a gift of chocolates and flowers or alternatively decorating a table and presenting the after dinner chocolates. The rim of the basket is decorated mainly with dried flowers and so can be used over and over again, whereas the small arrangements at each side use fresh flowers and can easily be replaced for each occasion. The chocolates will unfortunately have to be regularly replaced as they are bound to be eaten rather rapidly! You will need some glycerined copper beech or other preserved foliage and a selection of nuts, dried apple slices, canella berries, pine cones and a bunch of pink alstroemeria, 10 roses and about 15 large ivy leaves.

INGREDIENTS

Two small containers

Green florist's foam

A shallow basket, approximately 30cm (12in) in diameter

Glue gun and glue

Flowers, foliage, fruit and nuts, see above

Spray gloss varnish

Chocolates or sweets

1 Fill the small containers (I used cut-down aerosol tops) with florist's foam and soak well. Attach the containers to the basket. Using a hot glue gun, attach the copper beech leaves around the rim of the basket so that it is evenly decorated and the pots are well camouflaged.

2 *Glue on the selection of fruit and nuts to each side of the basket, filling the sides well to look abundant and interesting. Any nuts are suitable, but chestnuts are particularly effective, as are hazelnuts, pecans and walnuts. Once you have filled the edges of the basket, give the ingredients a spray with gloss varnish as this highlights the colours and adds an attractive shine.*

3 *Arrange some ivy leaves in the green foam, and add the alstroemeria flowers using a very short stem. Finally add in the roses, again on a very short stem. Make sure that all the flowers have been standing in deep water for some time before placing them in the arrangement. Finally fill the basket with heaps of chocolates or sweets.*

Photo frame & Dressing table posy

A photo frame is always a popular gift and the addition of a small flower decoration makes this frame even more attractive. The posy would look charming in any bedroom, whether the lady in question is nine or ninety!

$\mathscr{P}$hoto frame

A plain photograph frame can be enlivened by the addition of a small flower arrangement and the flowers changed time and time again. The small container used in this example was a brown aerosol lid but any other small and moderately inconspicuous container would be suitable. If the item you wish to use is a lighter colour than the frame then I would suggest painting it black or dark brown to help camouflage its presence. You will need only a small amount of flowers and foliage – if you do not have a garden then small pieces of house plant foliage would be a possibility. This example uses a few hellebore leaves, three pieces of conifer, a few strands of ivy, some larger ivy leaves and a spray of Singapore orchids.

INGREDIENTS

*Small piece of green
florist's foam*

*1 dark-coloured plastic
container*

Glue

*Plain, wide photograph
frame, 25cm × 20cm
(10in × 8in)*

*Flowers and foliage, see
above*

❧

1 Soak the green foam in water. Fill the container with foam and, using a strong glue such as a hot glue gun, attach the container to the bottom of the frame. Leave until completely dry.

14

2 *Arrange the pieces of foliage into the foam, covering both the foam and plastic container as much as possible. Place some taller pieces of ivy coming up the frame and others trailing to soften the arrangement. Any combination of greenery could be used.*

3 *Cut the spray of orchids into 2 or 3 pieces and add them into the arrangement. Make sure the foam is kept wet but not overwatered or it may leak onto the surface on which it is standing.*

Dressing table posy

Although posies and bouquets are perhaps thought of in connection with weddings and celebrations, they are also very pretty ornaments to have displayed around the house. This pink and cream posy would look charming on a dressing table or indeed elsewhere in the home. If you are unable to find a commercial posy holder, a similar posy could be made by wiring all the ingredients together. To make this posy, you will need a small bunch of eucalyptus (fairly small-leafed variety), a bunch of dark pink larkspur, a bunch of dark pink roses, and about 20 wired cream helichrysum.

INGREDIENTS

A posy holder

A frill to fit posy holder

Glue

Flowers and foliage, see above

❧

1 *Attach the frill to the posy holder with glue. Break down the eucalyptus into pieces of a suitable size. Arrange them evenly across the foam ball in* *the centre of the posy holder. Use as much eucalyptus as necessary to give a good covering to act as a base for the posy arrangement.*

2 Cut the pink larkspur into small pieces and push them into the foam so that they are evenly spaced throughout the arrangement. Do not make them too long or the posy will look straggly and untidy. Make sure the lace frill is still perfectly visible.

3 Cut the rose stems and helichrysum wires to the correct length and place the flowers into the posy. Scatter them evenly throughout the arrangement. It is a good idea to plan where they will go before inserting them in the foam to ensure that you do not have too many cream or pink flowers in any one part of the posy.

Get well soon basket

Nothing lifts a patient's spirits more than beautiful fresh flowers at the bedside. These fresh colours are a cheery reminder of spring, but an equally beautiful arrangement can be made at other times of the year using alternative flowers.

Get well soon basket

If you are feeling at a low ebb, recovering from an illness or just a bad cold, nothing lifts the spirits more than some pretty fresh flowers to brighten the room. Spring flowers are particularly cheering and lightly scented flowers help to perfume a bedroom or hospital ward but all flowers have a special magic! Make sure that you do not make too large an arrangement as space may be at a premium, and ensure it is easy to water and keep fresh. You will need a bunch of mimosa, a bunch of daffodils and some garden greenery.

INGREDIENTS

A small basket,
approximately
20cm × 15cm (8in × 6in)

Plastic bag or polythene

Half-block of green
florist's foam

Flowers and foliage, see
above

Scissors

Skewer or chopstick

❧

1 *Line the basket with a plastic bag (unpunctured) or some polythene. Soak the foam well in water. Wedge the foam into the basket, so that it is held in place. Using* *a selection of greenery, place some sprigs all the way around the basket and across the top so that the foam is completely covered.*

2 *Cut the mimosa into small sprigs about 12mm (½in) longer than the greenery, and place them into the arrangement. Any light, fluffy plant material, such as gypsophila, could be substituted for the mimosa.*

3 *To place the daffodils into the arrangement cut each one as you come to it, allowing about 2·5cm (1in) to go into* *the foam. Daffodil stalks do not respond well to being pushed into foam, so make a hole first with a skewer or* *chopstick and then place the daffodil into the hole.*

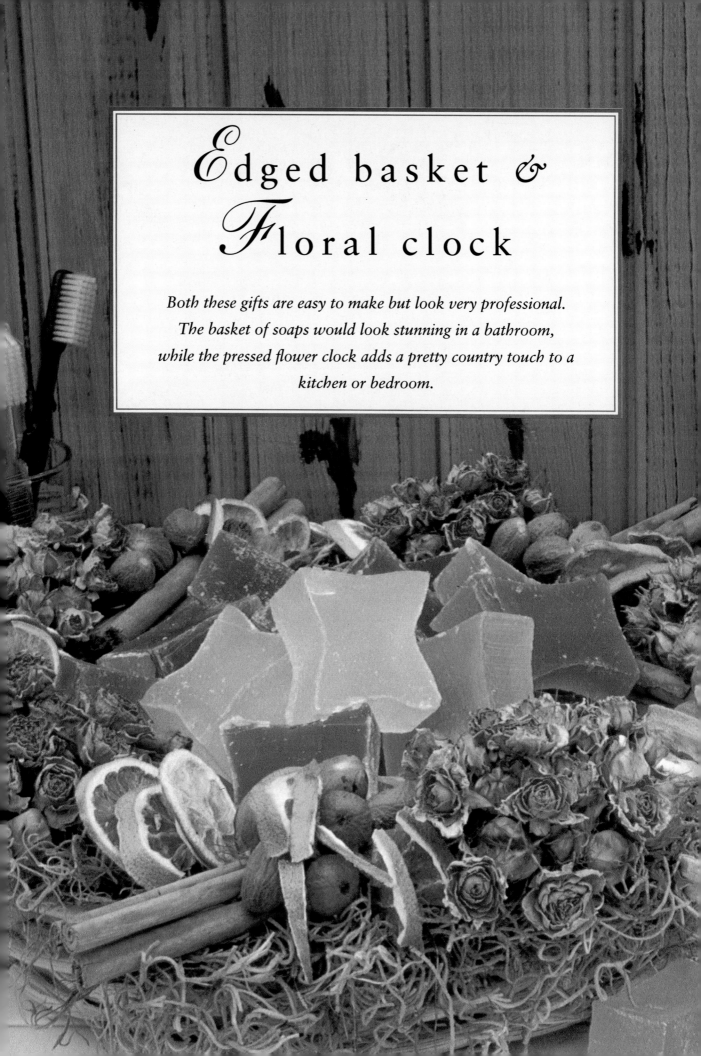

Edged basket & Floral clock

Both these gifts are easy to make but look very professional.
The basket of soaps would look stunning in a bathroom,
while the pressed flower clock adds a pretty country touch to a
kitchen or bedroom.

&dged basket

This edged basket would make a wonderful bathroom or cloakroom decoration; as an alternative to putting soaps in the centre you could fill it with bath cubes or pot pourri. If you wanted to give the basket as a hostess gift then it could be filled with sweets or chocolates. You will need a hot glue gun as using this is much easier than trying to wire the ingredients onto the basket. This basket used some Spanish moss, 15 sticks of cinnamon, 25 nutmegs, 25 slices of dried orange, half a bunch of nigella seed heads and 2 bunches of Evelien roses.

INGREDIENTS

Flowers, foliage, fruit and spices, see above

Glue gun and glue

A shallow basket with no handle, approximately 22·5–25cm (9–10in) in diameter

A reel of silver rose wire

Scissors

Tissue paper or paper doily

Contents for basket

ᏋᎧ

1 Make the Spanish moss into a sausage shape. Put some glue around the top edge of the basket and place the moss sausage over the glue. Press down, taking care not to burn yourself. Once the glue has cooled, use some reel wire to bind the moss onto the basket in a few strategic points to tame it and make the moss a similar height all around the basket. Glue on the cinnamon sticks in threes.

2 Glue the nutmegs onto the piles of cinnamon and then add the orange slices, some whole and some in halves and quarters. Other citrus fruits could be used, such as grapefruit or lemons or some dried apple. Then cut the heads from the nigella and glue them to the basket between the bundles of cinnamon.

3 Cut the roses quite short and glue them to the basket between the nigella seed heads. Line the basket with a little tissue paper or a paper doily and then fill the basket with pretty guest soaps, pot pourri, sweets or chocolates.

$\mathscr{F}$loral clock

Using pressed flowers to decorate a clock makes your gift a little more personal. But, before you buy your clock, check with the store that the clock will come to pieces, or it could be disastrous! You will need a selection of pressed flowers and leaves in complementary colours and of a similar size. I have used ballerina roses, pink larkspur and rue leaves with some small pieces of yellow solidago flowers.

INGREDIENTS

Clock with removable glass

Pressed flowers and leaves, see above

Tweezers

Tapestry needle

Latex adhesive

❧

1 Play around with the leaves and flowers at first to see what type of design you would like to do. Use tweezers so as not to damage the plant material. Once you *are happy with your ideas, you can start to glue down the design. Begin with the leaves as they form the backbone of the design.*

2 *Using the tapestry needle, apply a small blob of latex adhesive to each leaf. Do not put too much on at once or it may seep out. Here the leaves have been glued on in a circular design. Next add small pieces of solidago between each leaf.*

3 *Make sure each flower is well glued before proceeding with the next ingredient. Lastly add the roses and the* pink larkspur. *If you have put too much adhesive behind the flowers, carefully clean it off the clock face.* Then polish the glass and reassemble the clock.

Miniature spice posy

This little spice posy has a charming perfume from the cinnamon and ginger used in it and would make a delightful small gift or decoration. The cotton posy frill is a traditional backing used in German and Austrian spice posy work but another frill or backing could look just as effective. You can choose from many spices but it is important to have shapes that are moderately easy to wire and include in the posy. You will need 5 pieces of root ginger, 6 small pieces of cinnamon, 3 nutmegs, 6 sprigs of preserved ming fern, 10 small, dried pink rosebuds and 30–50 stems of dried lavender.

INGREDIENTS

Selection of wires

Spices, flowers and foliage, see above

22·5cm (9in) length of gold cord

1 reel gutta percha binding tape

Cotton posy frill, 10cm (4in) in diameter

Glue

1m (40in) each of pink and cream narrow ribbons

❧

1 Wire up all the ingredients except the nutmeg which will be glued into place. Cut the gold cord into three equal-sized pieces and bend into double loops and wire. Group the lavender into small bunches of three or five stems, depending upon the amount of flower on each stem. Cover all the wire stems with tape to neaten.

2 Make a bunch in your hand, binding wire around the posy as you go to keep the stems together. Spread the ingredients evenly throughout the posy. Slide the posy frill over the wires and push up to the base of the ingredients. Trim the wire stems and cover with tape to neaten. Glue the nutmeg into position and tie the narrow ribbons around to finish the posy.

Pot pourri

Homemade pot pourri is far
superior to the mass-produced, scented
wood-shaving collections usually found
in the shops. You can grow or harvest
all manner of natural plants and pods
for your mixtures, and long-lasting
fragrances can be achieved using
essential oils and orris root.

$\mathcal{P}$ot pourri

This selection of four different pot pourris representing the four seasons would make a wonderfully different gift at a very reasonable cost. Drying flowers and leaves for pot pourri can easily be done in a microwave by laying the items on kitchen paper and cooking for a couple of minutes on medium to high heat. Although you lose some of the shape, the colour remains, together with any fragrance. You will need four differing sets of ingredients – *Spring*: 10 lemon slices, 1 cup dried green hellebores, 1 cup dried delphinium flowers and 1 cup any dried grey-green leaves; *Summer*: 1 cup dark pink larkspur flowers, 1½ cups ivy leaves, ½ cup cloves and 1 cup pink rose petals plus a few whole roses; *Autumn*: 10 dried apple slices, 10 dried orange slices, 1 cup tangerine-coloured rose petals and 1 cup mixed beech masts and peach stones; *Winter*: 1 cup conifer leaves, 1 cup costus flowers (small pine cones), 1 cup broken cinnamon, 1 cup red rose petals and a few whole roses.

INGREDIENTS

Pot pourri ingredients, see above

4 mixing bowls

30g (1oz) orris root

4 × 2·5ml bottles of essential or perfume oils

Metal spoon

4 plastic bags

4 elastic bands

4 suitable containers

Glue gun and glue

1 Organize all your ingredients, making sure you have a sufficient amount to fill the four containers you have chosen. Mix the four ingredients for each season together in small bowls and add a quarter of the orris root to each one. Add the oil of your choice and mix well, using a metal spoon. Choose oils that reflect the ingredients used in the pot pourri, for example lemon oil for spring, and cinnamon for winter.

2 *Tip the mixture for each pot pourri into a separate plastic bag and shake well. Secure the tops with elastic bands and leave to mature for at least a week. The pot pourri mixtures can then be emptied into their respective containers.*

3 *These plain containers are ideal for pot pourri. They are inexpensive and easy to decorate for a gift. Remove some of the larger pieces from each pot pourri and then arrange them in a pretty group on the corresponding lid. A glue gun is a quick and efficient way to fix them in position but other strong glues could be used instead.*

Birthday sampler & Mother's Day basket

These delightful presents would be suitable for many occasions, other than those suggested. The striped design of the basket has a fresh modern feel to it, while the flower sampler is reminiscent of times gone by.

$\mathscr{B}$irthday sampler

This flower picture is intended to make one think of Victorian needlework and children's samplers. The time needed to make such beautiful works of art is quite incredible. The pressed flower version, although still a fairly fiddly project, takes considerably less time and a little less patience. Alternative background materials could be used, such as linen or canvas, depending upon your particular taste. The pressed flowers needed for this project are 3 ivy leaves, 7 small fern leaves, 5 pieces of alyssum, 7 sprays of freesia, 3 pieces of alchemilla and a selection of pansies, roses, potentillas and astrantias. Finally, you will also need a large number of potentilla centres – about 12 per letter.

INGREDIENTS

Wooden frame, approximately 30cm × 25cm (12in × 10in), with glass and hardboard back

Piece of 3mm (¼in) thick foam, approximately 30cm × 25cm (12in × 10in)

Piece of calico, approximately 30cm × 25cm (12in × 10in)

Tweezers

Fabric glue

Flowers and foliage, see above

Large tapestry needle

❧

1 Place the back of the frame on the table and cover with the piece of foam. Lay the calico on top of the foam. Using tweezers to lift the flowers, here potentillas, arrange the layout of the name that you want to spell, placing it either diagonally across the picture or horizontally across the middle. Once you are satisfied with the position of the name and shape of the letters, glue down the potentilla middles. Hold each flower with tweezers, then apply a dab of glue with a tapestry needle.

2 *Arrange the plant material in the bottom corner of the picture, by placing the ivy leaves on first and then adding the freesia sprays between the leaves. Place the pale alyssum against the dark ivy leaves for contrast. Add the larger flowers next and then the smaller ones like potentilla.*

3 *Then arrange the top corner of the sampler, again starting with the leaves to obtain the right outline shape. Place the*

smaller bits of alchemilla between the ferns. Then mix the pansies and roses together in the centre of the design.

Finally glue all the flowers firmly into position, applying the glue with the needle, and frame the picture.

$\mathcal{M}$other's Day basket

Although this flower basket is very different to the style of flower arranging we are all used to, its graphic design with stripes crossing the basket is fun to experiment with. You can easily vary the stripes by changing the colour of the contents or shape of the basket. You will need 4 or 5 hydrangea heads, 30 wired cream helichrysum, 24 heads of cream carthamus, a bunch of pink larkspur and 8 pink peonies.

INGREDIENTS

Long shallow basket

3 blocks of dried flower foam

Flowers, see above

❧

1 Fill the basket with the dried flower foam and wedge the last piece in to make sure the foam does not move. Start the arrangement with the peonies and place a straight row beneath the handle in the centre of the basket. You will need to have very short stems on all the ingredients.

3 *Complete the remaining side of the basket like the first, with bands of larkspur, carthamus, helichrysum and finally hydrangea. Insert these so that they overlap the basket slightly to soften the edges.*

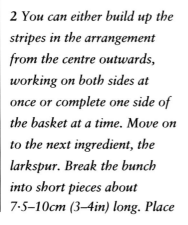

2 *You can either build up the stripes in the arrangement from the centre outwards, working on both sides at once or complete one side of the basket at a time. Move on to the next ingredient, the larkspur. Break the bunch into short pieces about 7·5–10cm (3–4in) long. Place a band of these next to the peonies. Then put 12 heads of carthamus next to the larkspur. Next make a row of 15 helichrysum, and follow this with a final strip made from pieces of hydrangea.*

Teddy bear ring

This enchanting ring would make a suitable gift for a young person or someone who is simply young at heart. The colours can be changed to suit the tastes of the recipient but any combination would be equally charming.

Teddy bear ring

This lovely little teddy bear ring would make a special gift for the little girl in your life and possibly for some bigger girls as well! Teddies are a perennial favourite and, although flock-covered bears have been used here, a small fluffy bear would also look adorable. You could make this ring with fresh flowers but it would not last for long; this combination of dried and preserved materials will last well if hung out of strong light. To make the ring, you will need a bunch of pale pink larkspur, some sprays of canella berries, half a bunch of green carthamus and some preserved foliage.

INGREDIENTS

Scissors

Flowers and foliage, see above

Glue gun and glue

Twiggy wreath, approximately 20cm (8in) in diameter

Mother bear and two baby bears

1 Trim the foliage into small sprigs and glue it around the wreath. Arrange the sprigs so that some leaves face into the centre of the ring as well as facing outwards. Next, glue on some preserved foliage around the ring.

2 Glue the teddy bears firmly into position, and hold them in place until the glue has cooled completely. Add in the heads from the bunch of carthamus. This is a very versatile dried ingredient as it has a good shape and fills arrangements well.

3 Then break the pink larkspur into small pieces and *attach them around the whole wreath. Finally, fill any gaps* *with some small sprays of the canella berries.*

Wedding spoon

Spoons have been considered tokens of love and luck for many generations. A decorated wooden spoon makes an attractive good luck token for a bride. Alternatively, by using less flowers and including spices and fruit, a spoon would look lovely in a kitchen.

Wedding spoon

Wooden spoons, such as the beautifully carved Welsh love spoons, are a traditional gift for a bride. Decorating a spoon with flowers is quicker and easier than carving one, and provides a lovely way to show your affection and wish good luck to the recipient. Although these floral spoons were primarily designed as a bridal gift, they could also make a lovely birthday or Mother's day present or good luck gift. To make a similar wedding spoon, you will need a few flowers and pieces of foliage – flowers from the garden would be fine or use a few leftovers from an arrangement.

INGREDIENTS

Drill

Large wooden spoon

Approximately 2m (80in) ribbon, depending upon desired length

Glue

Small green frog (attachment for use with florist's foam)

Scissors

Tiny cube of green florist's foam

Flowers and foliage, see above

❧

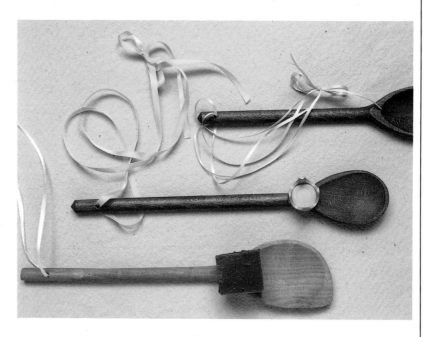

1 Drill a hole in the top of the handle of the spoon, either from front to back or from side to side, making sure it is large enough to take your choice of ribbon. Thread the ribbon through the hole and tie it into a firm bow. Glue the green frog onto the junction of the handle and the bowl of the spoon. Trim the prongs of the frog to make it *a little smaller. Impale a cube of foam, soaked in water, onto the frog.*

2 *Cover the foam well with some pieces of greenery; unusual bits and pieces such as catkins look lovely. Allow the foliage to trail over the spoon handle and bowl in a random fashion.*

3 *Add in some flowers. You will need to trim the stems to about 5–7.5cm (2–3in). Here I've used a small number of* spray carnations. Try to choose flowers that last fairly well out of water. Wild flowers never last well and *look much nicer left in the hedgerows, but many garden flowers would be suitable.*

Suppliers

For details of dried flowers, craft ingredients, and pressed flower ingredients and oils by mail order; also two-day craft courses on flowers and other crafts:

Joanna Sheen Limited
PO Box 52
Newton Abbot
Devon TQ12 4QH

For pot pourri ingredients and oils, and details of shops throughout the country:

Culpeper Limited
21 Bruton Street
London W1X 7DA

For details of dried flowers by mail order and farm shop:

Caroline Alexander
The Hop Shop
Castle Farm
Shoreham
Sevenoaks
Kent TN14 7UB

ACKNOWLEDGEMENTS

Jacqui Hurst and Merehurst would like to thank the following for lending props for the photographs in this book: David Robertson and Peta Weston for creating the special backgrounds; Shirley Dupree for lending the wooden toys from her collection; and Margaret Check, Hazel Hurst and Nesta MacDonald who kindly lent their lace, table linen and crockery.